1001 REASONS TO THINK
POSITIVE

Will the Real Women . . . Please Stand Up!

1001 REASONS TO THINK
P O S I T I V E

Special Insights to Achieve a Better Attitude Toward Life

Ella Patterson

A FIRESIDE BOOK   Published by Simon&Schuster

FIRESIDE
Rockefeller Center
1230 Avenue of the Americas
New York, NY 10020

Designed by Bonni Leon-Berman
Manufactured in the United States of America

1   3   5   7   9   10   8   6   4   2

Library of Congress Cataloging-in-Publication Data
Patterson, Ella.
1001 reasons to think positive: special insights
to achieve a better attitude toward life / Ella Patterson.   p.   cm.
"A Fireside book."
1. Optimism—quotations, maxims, etc. 2. Success—Psychological aspects—Quotations,
maxims, etc. 3. Conduct of life—Quotations, maxims, etc. I. Title.
BF698.35.O57P37   1997   96-29540
158.1—dc21   CIP
ISBN 0-684-83020-5

This book is dedicated to all those who have a zest for life, a thirst for knowledge, and a sincere desire to improve their own lives, as well as the lives of others.

A C K N O W L E D G M E N T S

In loving memory of my first best friends, Eddie Ruth Ross and Derrick "Big Daddy" Glanton. I think of you often.

In loving memory of my students, who inspired me to write this book: Corey Rowlett, Donald Preston, Broderick Burris, James Kelly, and Byron "Lil B." Norton.

To all of the Dallas–ISD Kimball high school students who encountered my teachings: "Don't Ever Give Up!!!"

To my children, Juanna, T'Juanna, and Martin III, this book is for each of you, first and foremost. Don't forget to take "the road less traveled."

To my dad, Herbert Jones, Sr., who has never let me down even when I let him down, I love you, Daddy.

To my brothers, I am proud of you all. Thanks for listening to my dreams.

To Evelyn (Muff): Take care of yourself on a daily basis.

Special thanks to Allen "Buster" Wilbon III, who stood by me when others didn't, and who taught me the true meaning of friendship.

To my literary agent, Jan Miller. Without a doubt, I believe in Jan Miller. Thanks for the support and constant watchful eye. Most of all thanks for believing in me.

To my Simon & Schuster editor, Laurie Bernstein, thank you for your guidance, positive reinforcement, and confidence in this project. By the way I loved the flowers.

To my friends Brenda Harper and Marva Owens, thanks for hanging in there with me.

To my publicist, Heidi Krupp, thanks for making work fun, fun, fun.

To Gladys Knight-Brown, my friend and confidante, thanks for the prayers. I owe you.

To Les Brown, my friend and inspiration. "It ain't over till I win."

To my wonderful newfound friend, Bob Asahina, thanks for having the insight and vision in the very beginning. I love you, Bob!

To Craig Gilliam, thanks for the education, and thought-provoking conversations. I would be less than a woman if I forgot to say THANKS.

HOW TO USE
1001 REASONS TO
THINK POSITIVE

RELAX: Find your favorite place to read and give yourself a few moments to relax completely. Take a deep breath, get comfortable, and clear your mind.

READ: Once you are ready, allow yourself enough time so you can really concentrate on each thought and insight, without feeling rushed or hurried. Then read each thought slowly and carefully.

THINK: Spend a few moments to analyze and consider what you read, and then repeat or paraphrase it out loud or to yourself. Understand the importance of each thought.

APPLY: Welcome each new thought and idea and then put these ideas into practice. Use them daily in your own life. Think of ways to strengthen and change your life.

INTRODUCTION

For as long as I can remember, I've yearned to put words, thoughts, and ideas down on paper—thoughts that I could come back to again and again whenever I felt the need. And so, each day I began to list everything that had proved successful to me and others. From the students I've taught, to the people I worked with, I've collected these deep and guiding thoughts.

After fourteen years of teaching experience and observations, I began to document those thoughts that seemed particularly inspiring to myself and others. Before I knew it, I had compiled this book, filled with thoughts and insights that I'm confident will help you achieve a better sense of self-worth and happiness.

1001 Reasons to Think Positive should help you find peace of mind, strength, and happiness in this sometimes crazy, mixed-up world. I hope that you will benefit from the ideas, lessons, and values contained in this book.

—Ella Patterson

1001 REASONS TO THINK
POSITIVE

Be true to yourself.

The best defense is also
the best offense.

Perfect is not an option.

Be a go-getter.

Dress for success.

Teach children right from wrong.

Discipline your child.

Love your children.

Surround yourself with friends
who "think positive."

Dance to the beat.

Help elderly people
for no reason at all.

Bring knowledge to your mind.

Give yourself an extra month each year
to reach your desired goals.

Have faith.

Enjoy your sensuality and your
sexuality before you enjoy sex.

Speak politely on
most occasions.

Talk to babies clearly.

Enjoy life.

Please your lover.

Share what you have.

Think positive thoughts.

Complete what you start.

Manage your own business
at least once in your life.

Hold on to your dreams.

Make the best choices.

Believe in your dreams.

Keep your promises.

Know what it takes
for you to be happy.

Write to old friends.

Let your enthusiasm show.

Pain knows no gender.

Make it a habit
to admit when you're wrong.

Keep in touch with old friends.

Bullies exist in all races.

Reward yourself
because you deserve it.

Everyone has
some type of prejudice;
don't let yours control you.

All things are difficult
before they get easy, so keep at it.

Maintain your weight
once you reach your goal.

When you want advice . . . ask.

Remember to celebrate your victories,
no matter how small.

Show up early for appointments.

Make business contacts.

Kiss your mate often.

Invest in something valuable.

Remain supportive.

The price of greatness is responsibility.

Enjoy your life . . .
enjoy your moments.

Notice the good in you.

Sit in the front row.

Sing in the shower.

Help someone who needs help.

Be a true friend.

Keep secrets
that were entrusted to you.

Smile often.

Hug a baby.

Trust your instincts.

Give more often than expected.

Cry sometimes, it's healthy.

Don't allow your stomach
to rule your mind.

Exercise regularly.

Speak clearly.

Count calories.

Stay in shape.

Whistle when you're happy.

Give those that you care for
honest praise.

Exercise your mind.

Set goals that move and inspire you
to continuously improve.

Read a good book.

Talk to your children often.

Refrain from stress as a habit.

Smile at babies.

Write a book.

Think happy thoughts.

Don't be a prude.

If you can't have it, let it go.

Spend less than you earn
and save the rest.

Read daily.

Discover a new hobby.

Remember short-term goals.

Don't be too busy to have fun.

Do something that makes you happy.

Think long-term.

Open up your heart.

Attach positive values
to each of your tasks.

Love something.

Start happiness from within.

Don't hurt others because
you've been hurt.

Recycle.

If you love yourself and what you do,
then you'll never really lose.

Act like a success
(even if you don't feel like one).

View your feelings as real.

Don't always expect to be right.

Say "yes" to opportunities that
you are genuinely interested in.

Be a winner.

Share your thoughts.

Respect yourself.

There is always something
positive that you can do.

Bloom where you are planted.

Keep your heart open to new love.

Pray daily.

Try harder.

Try to be understanding.

Stay out of trouble.

Drop all means of deception
from your lifestyle.

Spend quiet time alone.

Think before speaking.

Don't kiss and tell.

Adversity reveals genius,
prosperity conceals it.

Don't allow friendships
to hold you back.

Ensure that your innermost beliefs
support, enhance and
further your goals.

Encourage others.

Write down your goals.

Never sacrifice your health.

Take a self-improvement class.

Set aside funds
for having a good time.

Make love.

Discover nature.

Never stop learning.

Speak to people that you meet.

Don't measure success
by dollars.

Enroll in an etiquette class.

Relate better with people.

Network continuously.

Don't put off today's work
until tomorrow.

Get to know new people.

Admit the truth.

Be honest with yourself.

Learn to trust again.

Get the facts first.

Donate old clothes.

Don't feel sorry for yourself.

Sell your ideas with confidence.

Don't let anyone abuse you.

Take long bubble baths.

Recognize when others
are doing their best.

Know yourself.

Criticism is just someone else's opinion.

Write down good ideas the moment
you think of them.

Find things to be happy about.

Ask . . . does it really matter?

Give your very best.

Take showers and baths
with your lover.

Invent something useful.

Change your attitude
toward the positive.

Enjoy spiritual growth.

Find a cause to work for.

Protect yourself.

Stay alert.

Eat healthy.

Forgive yourself.

Men—even if you think you
understand them—never tell them.

Compliment people.

Don't abuse children.

Enjoy the moment.

Don't waste time.

Believe in yourself.

If you have a choice between love or
hate, choose love.

Visualize successful relationships.

Praise God first.

Praise others.

Forget the bull.

Use contraceptives.

Have picnics in bed.

Remember your first kiss.

Have candlelight dinners.

Brainstorm to come up with new ideas
and solutions to problems.

Don't believe everything
that you see or hear.

Be an unforgettable person.

Have a Sunday kind of love.

Don't be fake.

Take long,
thought-provoking walks.

Talk positively about
the man in your life.

Where there is no vision people perish.

Accept life as it is,
then try to make it better.

Do something that you like
better than anything else.

Show your love by doing
different things for your lover.

Help those who help themselves.

Don't let people put you down.

Develop a winning attitude.

Think of silk
when you touch your mate.

Volunteer for something
that will help others.

Remain open-minded.

Be creative . . . your creativity is the place
where no one else has been.

Dream.

Laugh.

Accept changes.

Think happy thoughts.

Know your own personal habits and
needs before starting a project
or assignment.

Look deep into your lover's eyes.

Change yourself for the better.

Cry.

Dance.

Don't smoke.

Bad attitudes
hinder positive skills.

Don't borrow from tomorrow;
live each day to the fullest.

Remember that you are a winner.

Keep pen and paper
with you at all times.

Don't be manipulative.

Pay attention to details.

Don't go off the deep end.

Work on improving your attitude.

Plan ahead.

Keep a calendar
with you at all times.

Wisdom is not a fad.

Good looks are skin deep.

Good performance is lasting.

Follow up on small things quickly.

Be critical of yourself
just as you are of others.

Mind your own business.

Be physically attractive . . .
keep up your appearance.

Be socially graced.

Add value to your life.

Don't be complacent.

Learn daily.

Don't be arrogant.

Purchase personal business cards
or calling cards.

Keep a journal to write down things
that will help boost your motivation.

Send birthday cards.

Let things happen
naturally sometimes.

Be a part of success.

Be a part of excellence.

Enjoy yourself every day.

Don't be late for appointments.

Don't be a complainer.

Push yourself toward motivation daily.

Avoid bad moods.

Control your weight.

Be open to new ideas.

Don't be afraid to change.

Be fair to others and keep after them
until they are fair with you.

Rejoice and be happy.

Be enthusiastic about the little things
in your life.

Get involved with your community.

Call before you drop by.

Use opportunities.

Be humble.

Carry change for parking meters,
pay telephones, etc.

Be yourself.

Program your brain to think success.

Improve yourself.

Strive for greatness.

Be fair.

Be nice.

Spend a minimum of three hours a day
improving yourself.

Search until you've met your goals.

Don't let obstacles get you down.

Tell good jokes.

Stay competitive.

Collect books; learn from them.

Resist both clothing and language fads.

Don't live in the past.

Get up early sometimes.

Be committed to your faith and family.

Reward yourself for personal
accomplishments.

Like yourself.

Work late sometimes.

Have breakfast daily.

If you must follow, follow a leader.

Follow, lead, and sometimes do neither.

Realize feeling sad
is only temporary.

Plan next week by this Friday.

Learn to do what needs to be done by
not indulging in self-pity.

Split up big problems into small sections,
and then tackle each section,
piece by piece.

Don't gossip.

Even when you feel that you don't need to,
check the want ads.

Beware of those who drop in unannounced;
they aren't considerate.

Be able to make clear distinctions;
it will help you to become more tolerant.

Expect excellence
from yourself and others.

Have fun in all that you do.

Don't waste energy.

Call someone whom
you've been out of touch with.

Don't take people for granted.

Celebrate happiness.

Be loyal.

Have a professional wardrobe.

Use the resources that are
available to improve.

Expect others to make appointments
with you when your time is important.

Choose effectiveness over efficiency.

Take your positive dreams seriously.

Overperform.

Ask questions.

Destiny is not a matter of chance;
it is a matter of choice.

Apply your knowledge.

Follow up.

Listen to the facts.

Don't depend on your memory;
write it down.

Don't procrastinate.

Understand why you want
to reach a particular goal.

Remain motivated.

Avoid negative labeling.

Don't fret over competition.

If possible, return calls
within one hour.

Don't slack up after success.

Strive to be number one.

Get to the heart of the matter
instead of wrestling endlessly
with gross exteriors.

Work hard.

Enjoy playtime.

Develop relationships with people
who are helping you develop.

Embrace every success along the way.

Your assumptions are the windows of your world;
clean them every now and then.

Don't let ego get in your way.

Develop good habits.

Be dependable.

Be responsible.

Dress conservatively.

Motivate yourself to do minor things.

Develop long-term
business relationships.

Turn knowledge into skill,
and skill into success.

Listen to people closely;
their buzzwords and yours
may not mean the same things.

Don't get caught up in your own biases
or prejudices.

Keep your breath and teeth
fresh and clean.

Change your situation
for the better.

Be as smart as you can;
but remember that it's better to be
wise than smart.

Keep clothes
fresh and crisp-looking.

Solicit criticism;
you'll identify problems better.

Don't overconsume alcohol.

Behave professionally.

Help your community.

Give people a chance
to earn your trust.

Don't confuse efforts with results.

Don't spend time worrying about the past;
move forward.

Enjoy the necessity of silence.

Don't talk down to people.

Don't give away valuables.

Don't overprice.

Don't underprice.

Learn from rookies, even if you are
a veteran at what you do.

Make your own fortune cookies.

Make appointments and keep them.

Learn something every day.

Put your "down-time" to better use.

Teach and enforce discipline
within your children.

Motivate others to do something
they desire to do.

Be persistent, not a pest.

Invest time in learning.

Don't think failure.

Don't train without learning.

Change for the better.

Sharpen your written
communication skills.

Have objectives.

Be positive.

Aim high.

Be consistent.

Create opportunities
and react to them.

Never cease to explore new ways and
new methods of improving yourself.

Be real; it lasts longer.

Budget your time wisely.

Get sufficient amounts of rest.

Never give up; have patience.

Measure it three times; cut it once.

Talk to yourself.

Don't shout to prove you're right.

Be aggressive, not oppressive.

Send your energy in the right direction.

Be sincere when you tell people thanks.

Don't get too relaxed.

Be practical; think practical.

Like a virus, wisdom tends to break out
at unexpected times.

Write a mock newspaper article about
yourself and the goals you've
accomplished so far.

Sharpen your brain with visualization
before you attempt a task.

Cash in on your success.

Effort has no replacement.

Improve a relationship
that needs improving.

If you fail, keep trying;
you'll find success on the way.

Take the first step toward forgiveness.

Show people that you can be trusted.

Don't be jealous.

The key to success is the driver of the car,
not the car.

Acknowledge your successes.

Life will not always be fair;
yours will be meaningless unless
you bring meaning to it.

Improve your speaking skills
by enrolling in a class.

Don't brag.

Don't keep repeating the same mistake;
learn and try a different approach.

Don't be a snob.

Pattern your actions so that
others will follow.

Think again.

Strive for improvement.

Imagine nothing; suspect everything.

Be mentally alert.

Change from the inside out.

Congratulate peers
on their accomplishments.

Take the time daily to thank God.

Be a builder.

Don't blame.

Own your feelings.

Don't bend the truth.

Don't deliberately hurt others.

Enjoy the ongoing miracle of life.

Deny denial.

Be realistic.

Thank your spouse
for help and support.

Take comfort in who you are.

It's up to you to create your own experiences.

Learn to live with differences.

Live and let live.

Recover from failure.

Schedule quiet time
for brainstorming.

Count and consider your blessings.

Keep your brain active,
motivated and alert.

Be a good friend.

Turn fear into faith.

Avoid name calling.

Think positive.

Believe that you are good.

Keep social and business
relationships separate.

Work hard at becoming successful.

You can do it, if you try.

Spend a quiet moment with God.

Expect to succeed.

Have faith in God.

Make time to do it right the first time.

Write a poem of your very own.

Find a mentor.

Handle your anger positively.

Understand your anger and don't
let it get the best of you.

Listen to music that motivates you.

Think and learn more.

Clean your body daily.

Romance men with your eyes.

Allow your dreams of success
to motivate you.

Be spontaneous.

Admit your errors; errors are human.

Get on a body-toning regimen.

Attend an inspiring church service.

Smile often.

Remember that everyone has a past.

Talk less about yourself.

Use Madonna tactics to succeed in
promoting yourself.

Conquer your doubts.

Don't be a spoiled brat.

Take responsibility for your actions.

Go beyond the call of duty.

Place spiritual growth
highest on your list.

Leadership is influence on others.

Ask for nothing in return
when giving gifts.

Excellence means doing your very best.

Don't ever stop striving for the things
you want in life.

Enough is not enough.

Smile seductively.

Laugh softly in public.

Love him in spite of all your
complaints and his faults.

Try to think as people around you think,
before you reject their way of thinking.

Women enjoy the happiness they give.
Men enjoy the happiness they feel.

Vanity and happiness
are seldom compatible.

There is a God; believe it.

Be a survivor.

Keep your friends close
but your enemies closer.

Children can be careless.
Women can't.

Pose the most motivating
question you can ask yourself
about reaching your goals.

Don't be personal,
but do be professional.

Don't apologize
for taking care of your family
the best way that you can.

Make a bet with someone who has
the same goal as you,
that you will achieve it first.

Get paid.

Don't lean
and you won't be let down.

The greatest art
of conversation is silence.

Thank that special someone for liking
you enough to stay.

Give yourself a pat on the back.

Know the King's English.

Don't go too far.

Learn from your mistakes.

Recognize beautiful moments.

Don't sacrifice comfort for fashion.

Put in twice as much work as it will
take to succeed.

Too often, just for us,
we want justice.

Temper governs the man.

Patience; always be patient.

Keep working to be the person you
believe you can be, and soon you'll be her.

Make a fun game out of
reaching your goals.

People who can't face reality turn to lies.

No matter who you are,
the rules apply.

Tackle your toughest problems first.

Take your time making love.

Know the importance of
living the moment.

Don't be well schooled in scandal.

Need a degree in psychology?
Keep living.

Love passionately.

Don't rush.
All things come in time.

Cherish relationships.

Nothing's guaranteed.

It's time to heal inside.

Deadline for complaints was yesterday.

Ask yourself powerful questions.

Be punctual.

People will forget how fast you did a job,
but they won't forget how well you did it.

Plan ahead.

Believe in your dreams.

Make time for your mate.

Thank a teacher who helped you
in high school.

Don't be a fool's fool.

Keep searching out your dream.

Keep working toward your dream.

Break free of abusive relationships.

Share thoughts.

Communicate daily.

Cherish wonderful memories.

Love is for sharing. Give warmth.

Don't be afraid to succeed.

Distance yourself from any negative
emotions you have about
accomplishing your tasks.

Don't meet disappointments
head-on.

Pick a motivating word for the day.
Use the word as a theme for all your tasks.

Don't get into the habit of lying.

Seek out opportunities.

Don't look for guarantees.

Raise your level of knowledge.

Remain mentally productive.

Nothing is scarce about God.

Nothing is what it used to be.

Change for the better.

Have hope.

Be assertive.

Grow continuously.

Be willing to give up the past.

You have to give up the way you
are to have it the way you want.

Be the reason, not the cause.

Be happy, rather than always right.

Don't be cruel to anyone.

Life is what is to come
not what already *was.*

Goals will create the strength you need
to build a solid foundation.

Treat others the way you
wish to be treated.

Don't agree to slavery
of any kind.

Happiness isn't materialistic.

The journey is life;
the destination was left behind.

Train people to treat you nicely.

Self-discovery is the first step
toward self-appreciation.

Think intelligently.

Make a smart choice.

Meet each other halfway.

Live until you die.

Write motivating statements on 3 x 5 cards
to encourage yourself.

Solve a problem.

Don't always agree.

If you don't change your beliefs,
you'll never change your life.

Embark on a weekend to energize yourself.

Find time to love what you want.

Lead, follow, or step aside.

Don't ever stop educating yourself.

Might be and
might have been
will become what is
if you worry about it.

Hope keeps all
suffering in its place.

Think again and again.

Find time to do what you love.

Make a choice so no one else
will choose *for* you.

Your friends are the people that your
parents warned you about.

Just be yourself.

Be happy or justified . . .
one or the other.

To have power, you must
be clear on what you want.

Accept the problem,
and you'll soon find the answer.

Keep the lesson;
throw away the experience.

Difficult times create suffering;
suffering will create change.

Constantly being mistreated?
Stop cooperating with the treatment.

Anger and danger
are in the same family.

Blessed is to get up one more time.

If you help enough people
get what they want,
you'll get what you want.

Try the unusual to find
your best strategies.

Acknowledge your unconsciousness,
and you'll awaken.

What can seem impossible is often
possible, with courage.

Work harder and be smarter.

What you don't use,
you'll surely lose.

We get more like ourselves
as we get older.

When how-to's become irrelevant,
you will have mastered life.

Attaching yourself to your solution
may become your next problem.

Donate blood.

Learn to trust.

Realize when you're hurting.

Visit the doctor annually.

Accept gifts without obligation.

You'll never "have it all together."
That's like eating once and for all.

Don't criticize.

Think and win.

Don't let yesterday rule today.

Not taking risks is a risk.

Comparisons tend to cause unhappiness.

If your aim isn't high enough,
you won't hit.

Trying to change someone
will make an enemy.

If you perceive it, achieve it.

Feel good about yourself.

Parents with undisciplined teens:
Keep praying. Keep talking to them.
Keep teaching them right from wrong
and most of all, guide them.

Walk tall.

Have a relationship before you have sex.

Make up your own games
if you don't like the games
other people play.

Ordinary people with extraordinary
determination create winners.

The bolder you are,
the more fortune favors you.

Don't be afraid
to lose what you have,
or at some point it will be lost.

Unload your ship
when it finally arrives.

Give compliments.

Honesty is not the best policy
if that's the only reason that you're honest.

Make good decisions.

Pursue worthy aims.

You can't solve your problems
by escaping from them.

Smoking in moderation
isn't possible.

Don't exaggerate;
it will weaken you.

Shared goals build unity.

If at first you didn't succeed,
you're normal.

Don't prepare for old age too soon.

Don't let anyone control your mind.

It's either reasons or results,
and reasons don't count.

Absurdity will have a hard time getting
ahold of you if you're already in motion.

Know how important you are.

There's no such thing as brutal honesty.

Be more natural than normal.

Don't make excuses for not doing,
or not having.

Blow your own trumpet
and it'll be even louder.

Prepare for life and live.
Prepare for old age and grow old.
Prepare for death and die.

Trust in your ability to live.

Get good at what you love to do;
you'll never get good at what you dislike.

There is no real way to know
before experiencing.

Starting at the top
only gives you higher goals.

Relax your mind.

Give people responsibility.

Sit with good posture.

Enjoy yourself in a life of your choosing
and a world of your making.

Remain rich in love.

Don't overreact.

Guilt directs people's resentment
toward others.

You are the only one who
can stop you permanently.

Confront who you are;
avoidance won't make it go away.

Don't spend most of your life
trying to prove yourself.

Invest wisely.

If you want to arrive,
you'd better start out.

Laughing last is not always best.

If you can't communicate,
you can't run your life.

Become 100% committed
to get what you want.

Don't allow your friends
to become enemies.

Watch your enemies,
but watch your friends more.

What works for someone else
may not work for you.

The best teacher is experience.

Ability x effort x results = winning.

Winning is an ingredient of success,
but you must experience loss to
appreciate winning.

It's not what you know that gets
you in trouble, it's what you
think you know.

When you are trying to become rich,
notice what kept you poor.

Be careful of what you allow
to happen to yourself.

Listen to soft music.

Losing helps create winners
through experience and fortitude.
You've got to hang on to life.

Believe that you can do
whatever it takes to succeed.

Open the parachute of your mind.

Have a taste of life.

Realize your potential.

Try your best to be potent, to do good
when you can and be brave enough to
live your life creatively.

Don't jump in if you don't like the
direction of the flow.

Two things come from fear:
inferiority and superiority.

God's gift is what you are;
your gift is what you become.

New experiences create new realities.

Communicate instead of
taking turns to talk.

Preparing to succeed is only
half the battle.

Seek the answer, not the problem.

It's not who you know,
but what you know,
when you are trying to truly succeed.

Failure is not falling down;
you fail when you don't get up.

Believe you are powerless
and you will be.

Don't get so big that you forget
where you came from.

Any good you can do
in this lifetime do now,
because you pass this way only once.

Sacrificing happiness
will cause unhappiness.

Accepting the fact that you lost
is a sure sign of a winner.

Being able to control yourself
is a sign of maturity.

If something needs to be done,
do it as soon as you notice it.

Do it right the first time,
to prevent having to do it a second time.

Accomplishment is not the activity;
it is the result of activity.

Don't major in minor things.

If you've given your personal power away,
take it back.

Allow your life to work
your way for a change.

You are the best teacher you will have.

Living positively
is not always easy;
you must be taught.

If you believe something is possible,
it will be.

Acknowledge where you are
and then move forward.

It's definitely too soon to give up.

Recognize your faults.

What you will do is what matters,
not what you can do.

Hardening attitudes is nothing more
than resistance to change.

Find out what makes you happy and do it.

Quitters will never win;
winners never quit.

Understand that
you are understood.

To grow old, keep living!

If you want to enjoy life,
keep living.

Don't continue to do
the same things if you don't like
what you're getting out of them.

Goals without time limits
are only wishes.

Don't keep negative feelings bottled inside;
once they've harbored awhile,
they hurt others.

Face up to your troubles
and handle them.

Willpower emphasizes winning.

Always seek the best.

Labor is stillborn without ideas.

Don't do cheap things to impress.

Follow your first thought.

Don't make idle promises.

Benefits come from
each failure or disappointment,
if you look hard enough.

What you think you know
isn't always so.

Your mind will work best when it's open.

Ordinary people have handicaps to help
them become extraordinary.

Weakening the strong
will not strengthen the weak.

Permanent change
will follow your lead.

Change your beliefs
to improve your life.

Walls that you've built within
are not steady enough
to keep you strong.

Don't do for others
what they can do for themselves.

Have a winning attitude
and good judgment is the result.

Believe in God.

Experience loans you some good luck,
but it should be used wisely.

Prayer allows you to talk to God.
Meditation allows you
to listen to God.

To describe others as they see
themselves requires tact.

Become the real you.

Healing brings forgiveness.

You won't win if you don't begin.

If you ask for rain, you've got to put up
with all the thunder and lightning that
comes with it.

Create your future,
but predict it first.

Believe until tomorrow.

Say that you need love.

Replace negatives with positives.

Recover for yourself first.

Let truth take its place.

Do efficiently
what needs to be done.

Let go of pain.

Don't wallow in self-pity.

Be with, be for, but not against.

It's okay to be assertive.

Try peacefulness when you feel angry.

Eat sensibly when you're hungry.

Many short-term pains
will produce long-term gains.

Don't do things for yourself
by using people.

Strive for peace within.

Don't believe everything that you see,
hear or read.

Rest, meditate, and then relax.

Forgiveness replaces bitterness.

Let go of negative thoughts.

Layers of resentment bury joy.

Learn five clean jokes.

To know a man isn't to marry him.

Don't break the law.

Don't give in to anger.

Execution comes first;
winning will follow.

Don't ask other people to do things for you
that you can do yourself.

Temptation is sneaky.

Think of all good things
as some good news.

Life's lessons are joy and pain.

Prayer is essential to recovery.

Meditation is essential to maintain.

If you really want to be smart,
learn to listen.

Recovery can't be fully explained.

Problems always look smaller after a
warm meal and a good night's sleep.

Your personal computer is between
your ears; you're programming when
you put garbage in and garbage out.

Our beliefs are based on others;
our dreams are based on goals.

Mistakes are lessons
to be learned from.

Believe that it can be done and it will be.

Don't spend time worrying over
things you can't do anything about.

Beliefs are investments
waiting to be improved.

You are a beautiful story
waiting to be told.

Don't let hatred
become your best friend.

The possibility of success
is sometimes difficult.

Have peace of mind.

Be firm, but fair.

Give the gift of forgiveness.

Spend time with your children.

Don't make choices for others.

Shoot for the moon.

Thinking it's too difficult slows or
destroys the possibility of success.

Affirmation
gets winning results.

Ideal weight feels better
than your favorite taste
(and it lasts longer).

You can argue for your limitations and
get a chance to keep them.

Believing in good luck or bad luck
is thinking like a loser.

Give yourself a gift
by giving your best.

Experts tend to know less and less,
so they continue to search for knowledge.

Never use the truth to hurt someone.

Upkeep will be difficult if your outflow
exceeds your inflow.

Winners make a life before making a living.

Horse sense equals stable knowledge.

Always try to be a good sport.

Have a goal or end up
working for someone who does.

When you can't afford it
even nothing is too much.

Take action to keep
from being depressed.

Trust and share.

Make time for yourself.

Solutions can be seen.

Allow God a chance to do the job.

Life is like history:
it will repeat itself.

Don't be overly dramatic.

Mirror actions
to see your true self.

Confessions are healthy for the soul.
To rid yourself of bad habits,
take off one layer at a time.

If you're lonely or discouraged or
unhappy, do something for someone else.
It will lift your spirits.

Don't commit yourself
if you can't do it.

If you need to cry but you can't,
peel an onion.

Your mind is a parachute.

Smile with your eyes.

Remember that your day will come.

Strength is stronger than you.

Listening is the first duty of love.

Mental malpractice
comes from negative thinking.

Continue to dream.

Trust the process of recovery.

Release feelings in a healthy way.

Honesty creates wealth.

The choice is the future.

A goal with energy
behind it is wishing.

Don't be afraid of winning;
winning isn't for losers.

Don't take over the marriage;
it should be fifty-fifty.

Just be quiet,
and answers will come.

Make peace with yourself and through
that peace you will share.

Don't just talk about recovery; do it.

Pay your debts.

Learn how to spell correctly.

Once fear is gone, healing arrives.

Don't allow abuse to trap you.

Move toward recovery.

Loving yourself will allow
others to love you.

Time to rid yourself of the addiction;
enjoy your life.

The best part about fighting
is making up.

Thoughts of love
should be remembered.

Fatigue is felt on a victorious day.

Find more than one thing
that works for you.

Find inspiration daily.

Have a variety for life.

Learn from failures.

Make a living will.

The future is never
as dark as the past.

Rise with the wind.

Do something
for someone who needs help.

You'll end up where you're headed
if you don't watch out.

Call a friend
who loves you when you're lonely.

Simplify your life.

Try not to buy cheap.
It's a waste of money.

Laugh at yourself
and begin to heal.

Use your knowledge as a tool
to improve your life.

A good heart allows you
to live a full life.

Forgive yourself; then make many
efforts to do better.

Success is the best deodorant.

Your misery may be
caused by your hatred.

Rearrange personal prejudices
and you're on your way to recovery.

Presentation is essential,
in food, work and yourself.

The door to your heart
is within your heart.

Allow ambition to soar.

Don't reheat arguments;
let them fizzle out.

Believe in miracles.

Pains produce gains.

Ride on a star.

Obey.

Willingness to give and receive
creates wholeness.

Take half the credit and half the blame
for misunderstandings.

Seek wisdom; become willing
to make amends.

The past has a guilty way
of surfacing.

There are 86,400 seconds in one day;
try to use each one wisely.

Make decisions in the morning;
that's when your brain is at its sharpest.

Easier decisions are made
in the counseling of God.

Share success with distressed friends.

If it doesn't interest you,
you'll probably be a good
evaluator of it.

Clear out space
by getting rid of fears.

Eat healthy snacks.

Your own strengths
are within your fears.

Self-judgment
can wear you down.

Blessings are derived
from challenges.

Act as if you will always succeed.

To aim for a legitimate business
is to succeed.

Trying to pick the lock
instead of using the key to success
is harder work.

Be willing to listen and
you'll receive answers.

Quality relationships
are needed as you change.

Do all the good that you can.

The best *you* can be
is almost good enough.

Get rid of ways
that you are withholding love.

If you must complain,
do it to the person who can help you.

The highest thoughts and feelings
are worth choosing.

Constructive praise is closely related to
constructive criticism.

Express yourself freely
as a part of having fun.

Asking for support
is the first sign of courage.

Give up at least one vice.

Others will hold you accountable for
your judgments.

Know when you've gone too far.

Don't be a thief of time.

Never quit a job before you
have another one.

Practice thrift.

Life can be changed
by changing thoughts.

Difficult times don't last
as long as difficult people.

Trying to see through people
will cause you to miss a lot.

Don't promise anything
that you can't deliver.

You'll make your life miserable
if you give up.

I.Q. will never be as strong
as I can or I do.

Tell and let go of
shameful experiences.

You'll get left behind
if you don't keep on changing.

Mom and Dad weren't always right . . .
they were human.

You're never alone
if you believe in God.

Peace, joy and love equal
real success.

Reacting to what life
gives you matters.

Big boys can cry if they want,
and men also.

Go for what's best
instead of what's good.

Simple things in life
create precious moments.

Others will appreciate
your gentleness.

Treat others as if you were the other.

Decide what you want to be,
then do what you have to do to be it.

Don't let obstacles
block your vision.

Don't compare
your life's dreams to others'.

Acknowledge God;
surrender to God.

Others will love you,
if you love you.

You get out of life
what you put into it.

Don't blame your mistakes
on anyone.

Failure is never fatal;
courage to try is what counts.

Imperfection
is the mother of haste.

Remain enthusiastic
about life's possibilities.

Everyone thinks
their load is heavier.

The only thing that's impossible
is what's untried.

Anyone who's always at her best
is a mediocre person.

Work to earn enough money,
not to work.

Little is accomplished
by overanxious people.

Everything
does not have to be your way.

Don't waste time
on verbal contracts.

Don't loan money
without a written contract.

Crisis represents
danger and opportunity.

Be able to make a living
from your hobby.

Old brooms clean corners;
new brooms sweep clean.

Be productive, but live your life
and have a good time.

Allow your children to grow mentally;
answer their questions.

Feminine instinct tells women what's right.

Don't be on strike
when your ship comes in.

You'll never know what you can do
if you don't try.

The oldest therapy known to man
is words of comfort.

Before you complain about your neighbor,
clean up your own act.

Criticism makes it easy to tear down
what has been built.

Handle depression like the sun does—
rise in the morning.

Appreciate luxuries.

Don't practice deceit.

Curiosity also kills ignorance.

Doubts should be kept to yourself.

Even wisdom is sometimes a fool.

Cheap talk is not free speech.

Change the subject
and change your mind.

Help others;
you'll feel better about yourself.

The greatest man
makes every man feel great.

As long as you are laughing,
it's considered humor.

Even though it is difficult . . .
sometimes give kindness in return
for being wronged.

There is no room for manly greed.

Hatred is ended only by loving.

Begin with the first step.

Love inspires kindness.

Send flowers to someone you love.

Old letters need no answer . . .
but are still fun to read years later.

Facts that are never heard are believed
less than gossip.

Listening is also
entertaining to people.

Money weakens the strongest fortress.

Mishaps either serve us
or cut us as we grab them.

The diary we all carry
is called memory.

Money makes money.

Music speaks in rhythm.

Optimists keep raincoats handy.

A job, big or small, is worth doing well
or not at all.

Bet on patience before power.

Leaping before you look
can be a big drop.

Think "success."

Practice personal obedience.

Ask God for forgiveness daily.

Prove your loyalty.

Help children.

Be afraid of standing still,
not going slow.

Handle your legal business.

Shave unwanted hair.

Doing often is good practice.

Don't forget manners.

Guide children
in the right direction.

Adopt a pet.

Watch a good movie.

Without a condom,
sex is group sex.

Jesus is well.

Give hugs that motivate.

Say I can, and believe you can.

Don't judge people
by the color of their skin.

Two places where the color of your
skin won't matter is
birth and death.

Stay in the best physical shape
that you can.

Create an imaginary opponent
that you can defeat.

If you are not getting where you want
in the time that you want, take a break
and find clarity.

Don't ever stop learning.

Keep souvenirs of your success around
your home or at your workplace; they will
keep you motivated.

Wear a T-shirt with a motivating
message on it.

Get started and keep going.

To achieve happiness,
never be caught without a goal.

Education is the difference between
what we are and what we want to become.

Pride shows in everything that we do.

You become successful by
helping others to achieve success.

If you ask the wrong question you
won't get the right answer.

You are doomed if you don't try.

You'll have to stick your neck out,
if you want to get ahead.

Scale the mountain if you
want to see the view.

It is never too late to be what
you want to be.

Opportunities are never lost;
they are simply found by someone else.

Ideas are one thing, but what you do
with your ideas is another thing.

Tie a knot and hang on when you feel
that you are at the end of your rope.

Knowledge is nothing without action.

To have a goal is one of the most
important things one can do.

It takes less to keep an old customer
satisfied than to get a new customer
interested.

The only true evidence of life is growth.

The only thing that prevents you from
reaching your goals is you.

An error is not a mistake until you
refuse to correct it.

Make your attitude a positive habit.

A diamond is a piece of coal that
stuck to the job.

All glory comes from
daring to venture.

If you want a rainbow, you've got to get
through the rain.

Even when no one else does,
believe in yourself.

It's your attitude and not your aptitude
that determines your altitude.

Failure is an event, not a person.

There is hope in your future and power
in your present.

If things go wrong,
don't go with them.

Regardless of your past, your future has
a clean slate.

Happiness is created, not found.

If you think you can, you will;
if you think you can't, you won't.

It's not the situation, it's how you
react to the situation that counts.

A strong positive self-image is the best
preparation for success in life.

If you have no plan in your life
it can't and won't go according to plan.

Set a goal to be the best.
It's more important than setting a goal
to be the biggest.

Expect to accomplish what you attempt.

The first two letters of goal are go.

Many goals create a fear of failure.
Lack of goals guarantees it.

A goal once properly set
is halfway reached.

C O N C L U S I O N

When trying to reach your goals: seize the moment by grasping at opportunities. Harness your passion, and keep your attention on the goals that you set.

Successful people are not necessarily wealthier or healthier than non-successful people. They don't necessarily have more education, friends, or opportunities. Successful people *do* lead richer and more fulfilling lives by doing what is more important and meaningful to them.

They live their dreams. This requires strong motivation to get themselves to do what they have to in order to succeed. In short, they know how to motivate themselves. This book is a reminder of those things that can get us all motivated. I trust and hope that you will use these ideas in the best way possible to improve your life. Enjoy these reasons to think positive.

Ella Patterson—writer, publisher, teacher, professional speaker, wife, and mother. She is a highly sought-after motivational speaker who hopes that you will benefit from the ideas, thoughts, lessons, and values contained in this book.

1001 Reasons to Think Positive provides inspiration for people of all ages.

Learn to appreciate yourself and the people around you, with a book designed to give you the most effective reasons to be the best that you can be.

1001 Reasons to Think Positive provides thoughts that help you live a rich and fulfilling life. This book challenges your morals, attitudes, beliefs, thoughts, values, and ideas, and it will challenge you.

For more information on Knowledge Concepts Educational Systems, Inc., or any Ella Patterson companies or products, call toll free
1-800-269-6228, or send in the coupon below.

RETURN TO:

Knowledge Concepts Educational Systems, Inc. (KCES)
P.O. Box 973
Cedar Hill, Texas 75104
or Phone: toll free 1-800-269-6228
Please send me information on KCES, Inc., lectures, seminars, workshops or products.

_____

NAME (please print)

_____

PHONE (business)   PHONE (home)

_____

ADDRESS

_____

CITY   STATE   ZIP

_____

Use ball point pen only.